BRIAN BLACK . J

Temples, Priests and Worship

Books by John Sharwood Smith

GREEK AND ROMAN TOPICS

TEMPLES, PRIESTS AND WORSHIP

JOHN SHARWOOD SMITH

Head of Classics Department, London University
Institute of Education

LONDON · GEORGE ALLEN & UNWIN LTD
Ruskin House · Museum Street

First published in 1975

ISBN 0 04 930003 2

Printed in Great Britain
in 11 point Plantin
by Cox & Wyman Ltd
London, Fakenham and Reading

CONTENTS

FURTHER STUDY

Αἰ δ’ ὅτε νηὸν ἵκανον Ἀθήνηξ ἐν πόλει ἄκρῃ . . .

But when they reached the dwelling of Athena on the summit of the city . . .

ACKNOWLEDGEMENTS

The drawings on pages 21 (4a and b), 23, 28, 30, 31, 38, 52, 53, 54, 58 were specially drawn for this book by Michael Reynolds. Those on pages 43, 55, 63 are from *The Antiquities of Athens* by J. Stuart and N. Revett (vol. IV, 1814), and those on pages 16 (1c), 18 and 19, 21 (5a and b), 26, 39 from *The Temples of Jupiter Panhellenius in Aegina and Apollo Epicurius at Bassae near Phigaleia in Arcadia* by C. R. Cockerell (London 1860). These are all reproduced by courtesy of the Royal Institute of British Architects, London.

The drawing of a terracotta model of a temple on page 35 is taken from *Perachora* by Humphrey Payne, and is reproduced by courtesy of the Managing Committee of the British School at Athens. The axonometric reconstruction of the Hephaisteion on page 16 is taken from the article 'Three Greek Temples' by W. H. Plommer in the *Annual of the British School of Athens* no. 45 (1950), and reproduced by courtesy of Dr Plommer and the Managing Committee of the British School at Athens.

The ground plan of the Hephaisteion on page 16 is taken from the article 'The Interior Colonnade of the Hephaisteion' by B. H. Hill in *Hesperia* and reproduced by courtesy of the American School of Classical Studies, Athens. The sectional diagram and the ground plan of the Parthenon on pages 20 and 57 are taken from the British Museum's *An Historical Guide to the Sculptures of the Parthenon* (D. E. L. Haynes) and are reproduced by courtesy of the Trustees.

The author is most grateful to Professor John Barron and Dr John North for reading the manuscript and for their helpful and constructive suggestions.

The priest and the silent virgin

A problem

A poet named Quintus Horatius Flaccus (who died eight years before the birth of Christ) ended a book of his poetry with a poem in which he foretold that his fame would continue to grow 'as long as the priest climbs to the citadel, with the silent virgin beside him'. By this phrase he meant, 'as long as the might and civilisation of Rome endure'. And this, he seems to have thought, was another way of saying, 'for ever'. If so, he was mistaken. It was about three and a half centuries later that the Roman Empire became officially Christian. The pagan priesthoods were abolished; the temples were destroyed or allowed to fall into ruins or turned into Christian churches; while the capital of the Roman Empire was now Constantinople.

Soon afterwards Rome itself was sacked by Gothic barbarians and from then onwards began a slow decay. The great palaces, law courts, amphitheatres, public baths and chariot-racing stadiums were deserted and crumbled away. Stones were prised off and taken to build and fortify the mean little towers that housed the quarrel-some nobles who supported or defied the popes during the Middle Ages. Shrubs and weeds grew over the mansions where the haughty aristocrats of Ancient Rome had been waited on by armies of slaves. Their marble statues were smashed and burnt to make cement, and their bronze statues were melted down for the metal. So perished the works of art that had been looted from Greece in the days of the Roman conquests – all save a few which were buried beneath the ruins of their owners' once-splendid homes. And so perished the might and civilisation of Rome.

Yet the poet's fame *did* continue to grow and his poems are now read all over the world. He is so famous that few people bother to use his full name. In his native Italy he is known as Orazio, the Germans call him Horaz, and the French and ourselves Horace.

But who was the priest who climbed up to the citadel? What was he going to do when he got there? Who was the silent virgin? And what did their climb have to do with the might and civilisation of Rome? The answers to these questions will be discussed in the later pages of this book. First of all, in order to study *Roman* temples and worship, we must look at the temples and worship of the *Greeks*. Greek civilisation developed before Roman. There were Greek temples in Italy when the Roman citadel protected only a few clusters of mud huts. And in religion, as in most things, the Romans borrowed many ideas and practices from the Greeks.

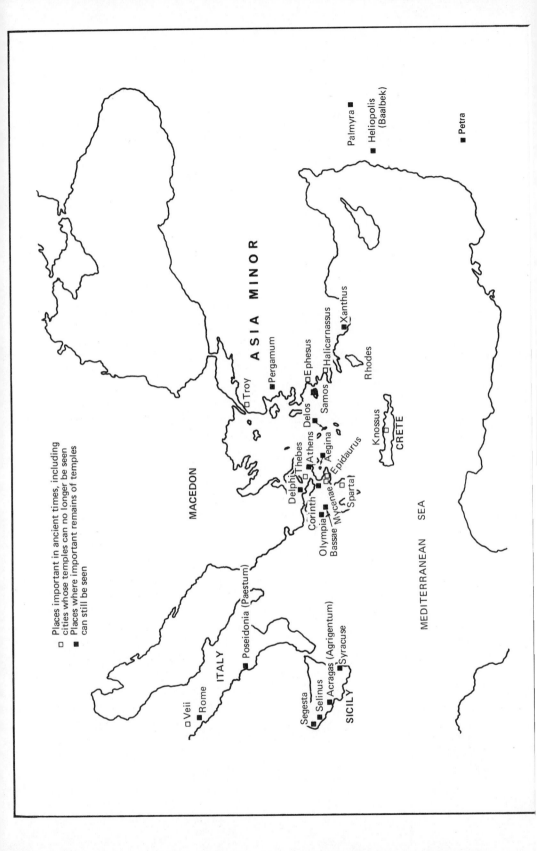

Places important in ancient times, including cities whose temples can no longer be seen

Places where important remains of temples can still be seen

ITALY

Veii
Rome

Poseidonia (Paestum)

Segesta
Selinus
Acragas (Agrigentum)
Syracuse

SICILY

MACEDON

Delphi
Thebes
Corinth
Olympia
Bassae
Mycenae
Sparta
Athens
Aegina
Epidaurus

Troy

Pergamum

ASIA MINOR

Ephesus
Halicarnassus
Xanthus

Delos
Samos

Rhodes

Knossos

CRETE

Palmyra
Heliopolis
(Baalbek)

Petra

MEDITERRANEAN   SEA

CHAPTER ONE

How to build a classical Greek temple

The commission

The first step is to get ourselves appointed architects in charge. If we are hoping to work in a democracy nothing can be done without a decree of the assembly of citizens. Such a decree would go something like this: 'It was decided by the people of Athens . . . to appoint a priestess of Victorious Athena, to hold office for life, and to provide her precinct with an entrance according to designs to be worked out by Kallikrates [an architect] . . . and to build a temple according to designs to be worked out by Kallikrates, and a marble altar.' (This is part of an actual decree, recorded on a piece of marble, much of which has survived to this day.)

The circumstances

In order to get such a decree passed we would need some leading speaker and politician to propose it to the assembly in a brilliant and persuasive speech. He is not likely to do this unless there is some good reason for building a new temple, such as the destruction by earthquake or fire of an old temple, or a great victory which has been won with the help of our patron goddess and has brought much profit to the state from booty and the ransom and sale of prisoners. The profit is important, as funds must be found from somewhere. Temples are very expensive to build, and fifth-century city states – even Athens – are very small and poor by comparison with the great monarchies of Assyria, Babylon or Persia (and much poorer still by comparison with modern states). Furthermore, although no waste will be permitted, either of materials or the workmen's time, we shall not be allowed to build on the cheap. To do so might offend the god or goddess whom we are honouring, and would certainly damage our reputation in the eyes of other city states which we all wish to impress with our great splendour and prosperity.

The contract

Because of the importance of strict accounting, the assembly will appoint a board of commissioners. These will draw up a contract with us, as the architects in charge, and with everyone else employed on the building operation. They will check carefully that all the work has been carried out correctly before they pay the agreed wages. They will have to present their accounts to the assembly every year, and if there is any suspicion of dishonesty or mismanagement some citizen is bound to think it his duty to prosecute them.

The designs

We would not have won the support of a leading politician for our temple if we had not convinced him that our designs will be good, and also that we can collect a team of highly skilled stone-cutters and masons and sculptors, and direct their work with efficiency. He will not expect the designs to be particularly original, or very different from those of any other temple. Public taste is conservative, and he and the assembly will merely want everything to be a little better designed and better executed than in any previous temple, with all the details approaching a little nearer to perfection.

The work force : social class and pay

If it is to be a big temple we shall need many more skilled workers than can be found in our city. We shall have to encourage them to come from other city states. From our own city we shall have to take all who are available, whether they are citizens, or metics (non-citizens resident in the city) or slaves. They will all be paid at the same rate for what they do (which is merely their daily keep and a little over), as will sculptors and architects. The architects will not sit in an office, drawing plans. They are skilled and experienced masons, not office men, and will, if necessary, turn their hand to most tasks on the building site.

If the temple turns out to be a very fine one, the sculptors and architects will receive much praise (and, no doubt, some envy and malicious criticism: envy, to quote Socrates, who was a stonemason as well as a philosopher, follows a great man round like his shadow). But neither sculptor nor architect will ever be considered a gentleman, since everybody in fifth-century Greece knows that no gentleman works at a trade. Trades do not allow those who work at them the leisure to cultivate their bodies and minds with athletics, dancing, singing and poetry; or to take an active part in running the state, as all gentlemen should. Nor will the sculptor and architect be admired in the way that poets and writers of tragedies are. Poets may be inspired by Apollo and the nine Muses, but the sculptor and architect, however good they are at their job, are considered to be just good craftsmen.

The work force : skills
For a large temple we may need up to 20,000 tons of stone, so skilled quarrymen will be required to choose the stone in the quarries and cut it accurately, according to the instructions of the architects and sculptors. Then, to work on the site itself, we shall need masons skilled in dressing stone and setting it in place, and sculptors for carving all the ornamentation on the stonework as well as the figures – if we are going to have any – on the frieze and pediment. Carpenters will be needed to build the scaffolding required to hoist the blocks of stone into place, to shape and fix the wooden beams and rafters of the roof, and finally to carve the wooden ceiling. If we have contracted for a new statue to go inside the temple, and the statue is to be a very magnificent one, we may need experts in working gold and ivory.

Some of our blocks of stone may weigh up to 20 tons, so we shall need experienced men to lower them down from the quarry onto special carts. Then teams of oxen or mules will be required to haul the stone to the building site, where other experienced men will hoist it into place by means of pulleys and winches as the building rises. But oxen and mules should not be too difficult to find in a country where the animals who pull the carts and ploughs are not always fully employed on the farms, and there will always be plenty of seafaring men who know how to handle ropes and pulleys. Each group of workers will work as a team, with a foreman who may be a citizen, or a metic, or even a slave. The slave will be paid the same as the others, though his wages will belong to his master.

The designs
Unless there are special problems to be solved, such as an awkward site, or the need to incorporate more than one shrine into the temple buildings, our temple will be something like the drawings on page 16. It will face approximately east, and in front of it there will be an altar, possibly connected to the temple by a ramp.

The site
If our city is an ancient one it will have an *acropolis* (citadel). Here, long ago, the king had his palace. It will be both the most conspicuous and the most sacred site in the city, where the oldest temples are. However, we may have been instructed to site our temple

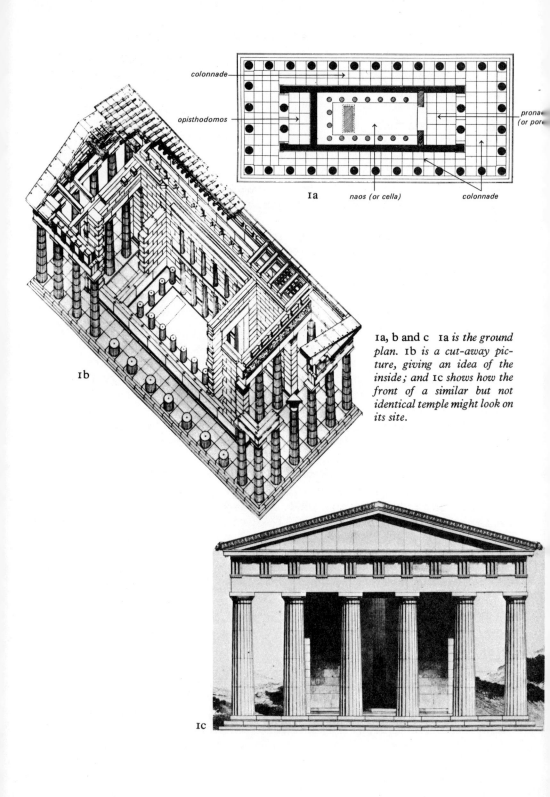

colonnade

opisthodomos

prona
(or por

1a

naos (or cella)   colonnade

1b

1a, b and c   1a *is the ground
plan.* 1b *is a cut-away pic-
ture, giving an idea of the
inside; and* 1c *shows how the
front of a similar but not
identical temple might look on
its site.*

1c

somewhere in the city below, perhaps overlooking the main market-place, or in a sacred grove some way from the city's centre. If our city is a colony founded within the last 200 years, it may always have depended on its outer walls for defence, and have no acropolis. Let us, however, suppose that our temple (like the temple of Victorious Athena mentioned in the decree) is to be built on an acropolis. We shall then have extra problems in getting the stone up to the site, but at least we shall have a firm base of rock to work on, unlike some architects who have to devise means of building a temple in a swamp.

The foundation and the platform

The first task is to level the site. If there has been a temple there before, as is likely on an acropolis, we shall economise by enlarging or otherwise adapting the existing foundation to suit our plans. On the foundations we shall raise our platform. This will not be completely flat, but slightly curved towards all four corners, so that the rainwater will run off. The slight tilting of the columns necessary to counteract this slope will add to the beauty of the effect they create. All the way round the platform there will be three steps. These will be in proportion to the size of the temple; so, if ours is to be a big temple, we shall have to add another step between each level and the next in front of the entrance. Otherwise the priest or priestess will not be able to walk out of the temple to the altar with proper dignity.

Columns, capitals and architrave

The next task is to put the base of the columns in place near the edge of the platform (see the ground plan of a temple opposite). The stone for the columns will arrive from the quarries cut in drum-shaped sections. Each (as well as all the other stone that comes up to the site from the quarry) will be cut about half an inch thicker than we shall finally need it, so that any scars received during cartage or during the building operations can be removed when the drums and blocks are trimmed back to their proper size and shape. Once we have made absolutely sure that the column bases are perfectly correct (it will be impossible to make any corrections later), we can begin to lay the foundation blocks of the *naos* (see the ground plan opposite). All the stones will have been marked in the quarry so that the masons can place them in the right order. We shall not proceed with the walls of the *naos* until we have completed the outer columns, which we do by hoisting the drums one on top of the other and fitting them together so neatly that the joints are all but invisible. Then, before we hoist up the architrave (the stone blocks that span the columns), we must place the bearing surface at the top of each column. This is the *capital*, consisting of the *echinus* and the *abacus* (see page 54).

Style and materials

Two important decisions will have been made right at the beginning. First, whether ours is to be a Doric or an Ionic temple. Second, whether we are going to build in limestone or in marble. If we have chosen the Doric style (our choice will depend largely on whether we live in the eastern part of the Greek world or the western), then the decoration of the temple will follow according to a strict tradition. If we have chosen the Ionic style, then we will have rather more freedom of choice. (For more information on these two styles see page 54.) As to our second decision, marble is harder to cut than limestone and shaping it takes much longer. This makes it more expensive, but because it is harder it can be carved to give sharper edges and finer detail. If we are working at Athens, we can get marble from the quarries high up on Mount Pentelicon. But if we are working somewhere else on the mainland, we will have to transport it by sea and land from one of the islands where it is found. It will be so expensive to do this that we shall probably be able to afford it only for special parts of the sculptures (such as the faces and hands of the female figures). However, if we do have to use limestone, we can give it a finer finish by coating it with marble stucco – a paste made of finely powdered marble. This process comes right at the end of the building operations.

The 'naos'

Next the walls of the *naos* begin to rise. The limestone (or marble) blocks come with projecting bosses left on their sides by the quarrymen, or deep grooves at the ends, where the ropes can be fixed to hoist them into place. The blocks are fixed together with iron clamps and dowels set in molten lead. No mortar will be used, and the edges will fit absolutely snugly, though behind the edges the masons will cut the marble back and leave it rough. At some stage we will need to give the *naos* and the *opisthodomos* their double doors of timber. If we can afford it we will perhaps cover these doors with a sheath of decorated bronze.

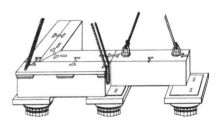

2a *Methods of lifting blocks of stone or marble.*

Pavement and inner columns

Now the pavement has to be laid and the inner columns raised. And before the timbers of the roof can be fixed in place, we must hoist up the sculptures of the *metopes* and frieze (see page 20).

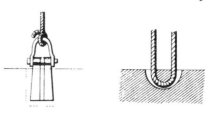

2b and c *Close-up of lifting devices.*

The sculptures

Everything will have been planned to a very tight schedule. No part of the work must be held up and no workman left idle. While the building has been progressing, the teams of sculptors have been hard at work on designs provided by the chief sculptor, who has himself put the finishing touches to the work wherever he thought it necessary. Their work must be ready to go into place at the moment when the masons and carpenters are ready to begin the roof, and as the heavy sculptured stone slabs are hoisted up, everyone will watch anxiously to see if they fit correctly. We can have sculptures in low relief (or even in high relief) running round the

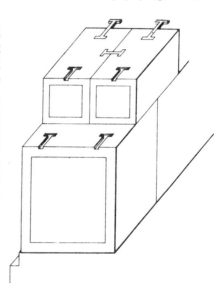

2d *This shows how the blocks were fastened together with metal clamps.*

outside, or even – though this is rare – running round the inside of the colonnade to form a continuous scene, like a very dignified strip cartoon in stone. And we can have sculptures in the round to place in the triangle of the pediment.

The roof and the ceiling

The roof will be tiled with terracotta or marble tiles, held together by overlapping grooves. As the roof has a gentle slope and the tiles are too heavy to be lifted by the wind, there will be no need to peg them to the rafters. Under the roof the carpenters will fit a timber ceiling.

PEDIMENT

METOPES

FRIEZE

3

The finishing touches

If a new statue of the god or goddess has been commissioned from
the chief sculptor, it will have been placed in position at the back of
the *naos* long ago. But it may still need the addition of gold plate
(for the armour) and ivory (for the flesh) to complete its glory. On
the other hand, if our temple is to replace a previous temple, there
may be no new statue, only a very holy ancient image to be reinstalled.
This might be a very crudely shaped lump of wood, revered because
it has been there since before the Greeks learnt the art of sculpture.

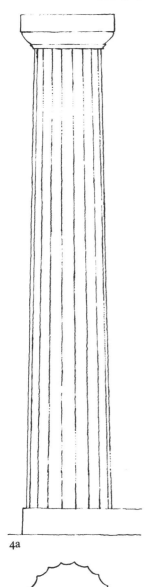

The shafts of the columns will have been fluted by teams of five or six masons, working simultaneously all round them, and will now look like 4a. The stonework will be trimmed back everywhere to remove the hoisting bosses and any accidental scars the stone may have received at any stage. The painters will have coloured the decorative features on the capitals and other stonework in reds, yellows and blues, all bright enough to stand up to the bright Mediterranean sunlight. The sculptures too will be painted. Human figures will be coloured – bronze for male flesh, or white for female flesh. Earrings for the females, weapons for the males and bridles for the horses will be added in metal.

At six corners of the roof there will be terracotta (or marble) figures of mythical beasts to show up against the skyline (see below). Along the sides, at the edge of the tiles, there will be decorative terracotta (or marble) spouts to carry off the rainwater.

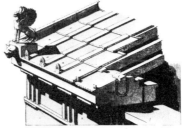

4a

5a and b *These two pictures show how the tiles fitted onto the rafters. They also show the terracotta figures on the rooftop and the terracotta rainwater spouts.*

4b *This is what the column would look like if you cut through it.*

Discipline and enthusiasm

The whole task will have taken anything from six to fifteen years, depending on the size of the temple, the efficiency of the planning and the keenness of the workers. We may have needed up to a thousand men altogether, and up to two hundred men working on the site at any one time. The state commissioners will have been kept busy checking that no precious materials have been stolen, or any blocks damaged through carelessness. They may have to interfere to check rivalries between teams of workmen from different cities, which might easily turn into time-wasting – or even dangerous – quarrels.

However, everyone engaged on building a temple should be working for something more than his rather meagre pay. He will have watched a glorious building rise from its foundations, knowing that he was playing a part, however modest, in its construction, and that the god (or goddess) for whom it was intended was undoubtedly taking a delighted interest in the construction of his house. There is a story told about the building of a ceremonial gateway to the sacred precinct on the Acropolis at Athens: one of the workmen, the keenest and most hard-working of all, slipped and fell from a great height, and was so badly injured that the doctors expected him to die. But Pericles, the Athenian statesman who had proposed the construction of the building, had a dream in which the goddess Athena appeared to him and told him exactly how the workman could be cured. And so he was.

The style

Except for the gently sloping roof, all the lines of our building have been either vertical or horizontal. There have been no arches, domes or vaults. Rather a dull building, you might think. The sort of building a child might design with a box of toy bricks. Very humdrum when compared to the soaring splendour of a Gothic cathedral, or to a triumph of modern architectural engineering such as the Sydney Opera House. The first Greek stone temples were certainly solid, and very likely dull. However, this design pleased the Greeks – a rectangular *pronaos*, *naos* and *opisthodomos*, with a portico in front and a colonnade (sometimes a double colonnade) of fluted columns running all round. It was copied in all parts of the Greek world, and for two centuries it was considered to be more or less the only way to build a temple. By working continuously to perfect this one design (instead of experimenting with new designs), by combining massiveness with light and space, and by their superb workmanship, the Greek masons succeeded eventually in constructing buildings of astonishing beauty.

The Parthenon

The greatest achievement in the art of temple building was the temple built for Athena on the Acropolis at Athens between 447 and 432 BC, known to us as the Parthenon. It is no exaggeration to say that, with all our resources in technology, it would be quite impossible to construct such a building today. And most modern architects are agreed that it must have been the most beautiful building ever erected.

6 *A reconstruction of the Parthenon giving some idea of how it may have looked.*

CHAPTER TWO

Priests, sacrifice and worship

Precinct, temple and altar

For a Greek community to worship its gods, three things were desirable: a sacred precinct, a temple and an altar. But of these the altar alone was essential. The precinct was a piece of ground marked out in such a way that anyone would know when he was stepping onto land that belonged to a god. It had to be large enough to accommodate all the congregation in such a way that each person could see the altar. This was always in the open air (usually at the east end of the temple), and the act of worship was a sacrifice, usually presided over by a priest or priestess, though this was not always necessary. The temple was not essential either: there were some important altars that had no temple. The one vital and awe-inspiring object in Greek worship was the altar.

What was the temple for?

The answer to this question is quite simple. It was a house for the god to live in. We might think it strange and foolish for anyone to suppose that a god whom no one ever saw – except in dreams like that of Pericles (page 22) – should need to live in a house built by the hands of men. However, we must remember that people living in pre-technological societies are very conscious of their weakness in the face of the catastrophes of nature, such as storms, earthquakes, famines and epidemics, and of their dependence on the fertility of their flocks and fields. Their lives, much more than ours (with our social security and insurance policies), are at the mercy of good and ill luck. So it was easy for the Greeks to feel that behind their experiences of pain or joy lay the activities of beings with needs and natures like their own, but invisible and immortal and gifted with stupendous power. Through being members, however insignificant, of a vast, co-operative, technological enterprise, *we* enjoy, unless we are very unlucky, comfort and security and great power over our environment. But the Greek villager shivered in winter and baked in summer, lived on meagre rations, went to bed at dusk (for lack of artificial light) and got up at dawn, and depended on his own legs for getting from one place to another (if indeed he could afford the time to go anywhere).

So it is only in rare moments – if we should be lost and alone in jungle or desert, or confronted by some crushing personal tragedy – that we come to realise that although our scientific education has taught us *how* earthquakes and famines, fertility and childbirth, disease and death, come about, it has not told us *why*. Awareness of that unanswered question led the Greeks to feel themselves surrounded by works of nature full of awe and wonder, and to wish to express by acts of worship their feelings of gratitude and reverence towards whatever powers might control those works of nature. And the best way of worshipping they knew was to offer to the gods the things they themselves took pleasure in – beautiful sculpture, splendid buildings and succulent feasts. There was much more to Greek religion, of course, but this is perhaps enough to suggest how a house for the god, and an altar to sacrifice on, could seem an important part of city life. Later, as the Greeks became more confident of their ability to control their own lives, and more inclined to use their reasoning powers, the more sophisticated of them no longer imagined that the god actually lived in the temple. They merely thought that a beautiful temple was a good way to honour him (and to show neighbouring cities that you could build more beautifully than they could). It was also a conveniently safe place to store, under the protection of the god, all the precious offerings made to him (which might be borrowed by the state in time of need). Besides, it made a suitable place for fine statues, an inspiring setting for the great religious festivals of the state, and a heartening sight to glimpse as you went about business, or leisure, in or near the city.

What happened inside a Greek temple?
Very little. The *naos* housed the statue of the god, the *pronaos* housed the more impressive of the offerings made to him, and the *opisthodomos* housed the rest of the offerings, along with the treasure that had accumulated from the sale of the skins of the sacrificed animals, and the profit from loans made at interest. When the double doors were opened on the occasion of a sacrifice, the god looked out at the ceremony and smelt the odour of burnt offerings. The public did not enter the *naos* to worship – there was no altar inside the temple – but they may have gone there to admire the statue. There were no windows in the *naos*, so the interior would be dark except for the

7 *This is a Victorian artist's idea of what the inside of a Greek temple looked like. It is based on studies made by the artist on the site of the temple of Apollo at Bassae. The frieze shown between the top of the pillars and the ceiling can be seen in the British Museum.*

flickering light from oil lamps, and the reflected light that came in through the door from the strong sunlight outside. The only persons who had business in the *naos* were the priest (or priestess) and the temple attendants.

What happened outside a Greek temple?
All the important ceremonies connected with the worship of the god. The most important of these were the state sacrifices conducted at the altar. In establishing a priesthood the assembly might decree that the priest should conduct a sacrifice to the god on behalf of the state at fixed intervals, once a month perhaps, or once a year. There would be other ceremonies concerned with the cult statue. This would not be the beautiful new statue carved by a famous sculptor, but a clumsily made image, so ancient that no one knew where it had come from, which was venerated in the same way that relics of saints and martyrs are venerated now in some Italian or Spanish churches. The cult statue might be ceremonially carried out of its shrine from time to time, to be washed in a stream or in the sea. On other occasions it might be presented with a new robe.

The Panathenaic procession
Every four years there was a great festival at Athens, called the *Panathenaea*, which was held in honour of the patron goddess who protected the city – 'for ever and ever', in the words of an Athenian poet and statesman. It lasted four days and included dancing, singing, torch races, recitation of the Homeric poems, and also athletic contests and musical competitions in which Greeks from outside Athens were allowed to compete. But the most important part of the proceedings was a great procession through the city, in which leading citizens, metics, allies, young women from the best families, and all other citizens who wished, paraded on foot, or in cavalcade, to the Acropolis. At the head of the procession was carried an elaborate robe, woven over a period of nine months by girls chosen from the most aristocratic families. This robe was ceremonially presented by the priestess to the ancient wooden image of Athena, which lived, not in the Parthenon, but in another temple on a far older and holier site. In the procession went animals for sacrifice at the great altar of Athena – a slab of natural rock on the south side of the Parthenon. The drawings on page 28 show some of the sections of a great frieze which decorated the Parthenon and depicted incidents in the procession.

Priests and priestesses
The gods were usually served by priests and goddesses by priestesses.

8a and b

These were ordinary citizens who had been elected to a priesthood, or had been chosen by lot (or even in some cases had bought their priesthood). For some priesthoods it was necessary to belong to one particular family, and for some only unmarried girls were eligible; they had to give up their priesthood when they married. Being a priest or priestess was not a full-time occupation, and required no special training, except that the priest or priestess had to know all the rituals required at his or her particular temple. It was not necessary to be specially religious. But it was necessary to have no physical defects, and if the priest or priestess was married and had children, and one of these children died, he or she would have to give up the priesthood.

The duties of priests and priestesses
They presided at all state sacrifices, though they did not have to kill the sacrificial victims themselves. Their task was to make sure that the correct ritual was followed, and to say the correct prayers at the correct moment. It was also their duty to supervise the ceremonial washing and robing of the statue. With the help of the temple attendants (some of whom might be slaves owned by the god) they

were responsible for the care of the temple building and the precinct, and they had to see that nothing happened in it that was improper. When, at the end of the sixth century BC, a Spartan king invaded Athens in support of some Athenian nobles and wanted to make his headquarters on the Acropolis, he was at once met by the priestess and sternly told to go away. It was not proper, she said, for a Dorian to set foot in the sacred precinct of the goddess. (Spartans were members of the Dorian, and Athenians of the Ionian branch of the Greek-speaking peoples.) The king claimed that the Spartan royal family were not Dorians, and refused to depart. Soon afterwards he was besieged in the precinct by other Athenians and had to surrender ignominiously. He had got what he deserved for disobeying a priestess in her precinct.

The temple commissioners
These would be a small board of citizens, appointed by the state to look after the revenues of the temple and to supervise the upkeep of the buildings.

The rewards of a priesthood
In the first place it was a great honour: how great an honour depended on the importance of the temple. It might bring the priest (or priestess) special privileges, such as a place of honour in religious processions, or special seats at dramatic festivals. Secondly, it would be lucrative, in a small way. The priest (or priestess) was often entitled to a part of the profits from the sale of the skins of the sacrificial animals, or of the perishable offerings such as fruit, honey, oil or vegetables.

The altar
Just before the sacrifice took place the priest or priestess uttered a prayer, inviting the god to be present to accept the sacrifice, and there was a strong and persistent feeling that at the solemn moment of the death of the victim the god *was* there. An altar was therefore a specially sacred object, and for this reason no one, neither criminal nor political enemy, must ever be subjected to violence if he had taken refuge at an altar. If this should happen the consequences might be terrible.

When the sacrificial victim reached the altar, it, and the priest who consecrated it, and the congregation who stood within the sacred precinct, were felt, if the sacrifice was successful, to be for a moment united with the god in a mysterious bond.

An altar could be very simple – a turf mound; a slab of natural rock with a flat surface at the right height, like the one on the Athenian

Acropolis; the heaped-up ashes of victims killed and burnt over many years. Or it could be a slab of carved marble with steps and a platform, such as the altar the Athenians proposed to raise in front of Kallikrates' temple to Victorious Athena. If the temple was an important one the altar would have to be large enough for as many as a hundred oxen to be sacrificed at a time; and there would have to be a large gutter to carry away the blood.

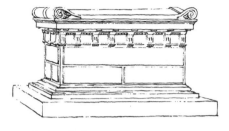

9 *A carved altar.*

Sacrifice

When presiding over a sacrifice the priest would wear the long, dignified tunic which had once been the normal dress for everyone. He wore a woollen band round his head (white for Olympian gods, purple or black if the temple were dedicated to the gods of the Underworld). Wool, being one of the most ancient products of the labours of man, was thought to have a special sanctity. The priest stood with his back to the temple, the doors of which stood wide open so that the god (that is to say his statue) could watch the ceremony. The priest would pronounce the correct invocations and perform any necessary ritual acts, such as dipping a smouldering length of wood from the altar in a bowl of water and sprinkling it over the congregation to purify them, or cutting a piece of the victim's hair and placing it on the altar to symbolise its dedication to the god. If the temple was sacred to a goddess the victim offered would be female, if the offering was being made to the gods of the Underworld the victim would be black. Certain animals were suitable for particular gods: horses for Poseidon or for the sun god, Helios; black dogs for Hekate, the goddess of the Underworld; asses for Apollo. Before being led to the altar the animals might be adorned with garlands, and if they had horns these might be gilded to make them a more precious offering. The drawing opposite is of one of the sections of the frieze showing the Panathenaic procession. One of the heifers is being led to be sacrificed on the Acropolis.

At the proper moment the official sacrificer would stun the animal and skilfully cut its throat, holding its head up to the sky if it was being offered to an Olympian god, but towards the earth if it was intended for a god of the Underworld. Then it would be cut up and certain portions placed on the altar to be burnt, and the rest roasted for the priest and the congregation to share.

10

The significance of sacrifice

For the Greeks, who lived so much nearer to famine and starvation than we do, eating and drinking were an occasion to remember the gods on whom humans depended for the produce of nature. A family would not take a meal together without the father sprinkling a few drops of wine to the gods, any more than a Victorian family would sit down to a meal without the father saying grace. On innumerable occasions of private life – on the eve of a voyage or a business deal, or after the harvest, or in gratitude for some personal success or recovery from an illness – a small sacrifice would be made by an individual or a group of people at one of the many shrines in the city or countryside. The great state sacrifices, at which the offerings were made on behalf of everyone, were solemn and patriotic occasions and no doubt very moving, as is often the case when a great crowd comes together united in a common purpose.

To us blood sacrifice seems repulsive and absurd. We do not like seeing animals slaughtered. This does not stop most of us from eating lamb, beef or pork, but we arrange for the animals to be slaughtered out of sight in a slaughterhouse. We have been taught to despise the idea that God might be pleased with the gift of part of a slaughtered animal (an attitude we owe to the first Christians, who learnt it from the Jews – though the Jews had not always felt this way, as we are reminded in the story of Abraham and Isaac). But to the ordinary Greek citizen a blood sacrifice did not seem an act of unnecessary cruelty. It was a moment for forgetting wordly affairs, and brought honour to the god, to the victim and to those who offered the victim.

Not all Greek sacrifices were blood sacrifices. Offerings were also made of vegetables and fruits (like the Christian harvest festival) and of honey, milk and oil. Some altars were reserved for bloodless sacrifices, and were called 'pure'. Not quite all Greeks approved of blood sacrifice. One philosopher attacked the idea that such a sacrifice was a proper way to atone for the killing – accidental or deliberate – of a fellow human being. He said that to wash blood away by blood was like attempting to clean mud away with mud.

CHAPTER THREE

Greek temples – origins and early development

Minoans and Mycenaeans

Before the classical Greek civilisation there was another civilisation in Greece (called Mycenaean), and before that yet another on the island of Crete (called Minoan). Much about these two civilisations is still a mystery, but it is clear that somehow they merged together and somehow they both collapsed about 1,200 years before the birth of Christ. During the later stages of this pre-classical civilisation the mainland of Greece had been ruled by Greek-speaking kings who lived in imposing palaces, some of them strongly fortified and perched on the top of hills or crags which were well suited to defence. At the foot of these crags, which later Greeks called *acropoleis*, had clustered the dwellings of the common folk. With no literary evidence surviving, it is very difficult to discover much about the religious ideas and practices of this period. There is good reason to suppose that gods were thought to inhabit certain caves and mountain tops, and some reason to suppose that the king lived and ruled under the protection of a goddess who had taken his family and his city under her special care. This goddess he perhaps worshipped in a private shrine in his palace. In the Minoan–Mycenaean civilisation the king was everything. Regarded as so far above other people that he was almost a god himself, he led the people in war; he made the laws and judged disputes; and when the people needed the help of the gods in time of famine or pestilence or other danger, it was to the king that they turned to pray for them.

The dark age

During the collapse of the Mycenaean civilisation the kings and their nobles were driven out, fled overseas or were killed, and their palaces were sacked and burnt. A new invasion of Greeks had come from the north. They moved across Greece in their tribes, destroying as they went. Eventually they occupied all the most fertile parts of Greece and forced the common people, who had remained behind when the nobles fled, to work the land as serfs, so that they themselves could be free to spend their lives fighting and hunting. Athens alone was unconquered and seems to have welcomed many fugitives from the conquered areas. Some of them stayed, others crossed the sea eastwards to found colonies on the islands and coasts of Asia Minor. Nor were these the only colonies founded at this time. Some of the invaders who could not find enough land left in mainland Greece also took to the seas and found other islands and other coastal sites to colonise. They mostly went westwards to Italy and Sicily. Most of these colonists seized land that was already occupied and built themselves towns to settle in so that they could defend themselves against the hostility of the previous inhabitants. Because of colonisation the culture of the Greeks spread to many places outside Greece.

The first beginnings of Greek civilisation
After several generations of confusion and constant fighting, the invaders began to form small towns by joining together the villages in which they had settled. These little towns were the beginnings of the city states of the fifth century. They were built of sun-dried mud bricks, with narrow winding streets and houses higgledy-piggledy, and at first they had no walls. Some of them, however, were near one or other of the old Mycenaean citadels, and to these the inhabitants could flee for refuge when they were attacked by pirates or other enemies.

From kings to aristocracies
At some time during the Dark Ages nearly all the Greek communities got rid of their kings and chieftains, and instead were ruled by a few noble families. All the duties the king had performed were now divided among these families. One man led the people in war, others made the laws and acted as judges, and others took over the king's duties in religion. Though the nobles had houses in the towns, they still owned farms in the countryside, and many of the humbler citizens still lived in country villages, though they came to the town to market, or for lawsuits, or to muster in time of war. In the villages they still worshipped at their tribal shrines and at the tombs of their ancestors, but, as they came to feel a dependence on their fellow citizens and a loyalty to their town, they also began to feel the need for a goddess to watch over them all. The religion of the old civilisation had not disappeared, but had become mingled with the religion the invaders had brought with them, so that the two had become indistinguishable.

The first temples

When the old palaces had been burnt down and abandoned, the goddess who had protected the king, and through the king his people,
had lost her home. So if the people in the town were not to be unpro-
tected, a new house would have to be built for her.

In the Dark Ages the arts of building had been lost, and neither
the nobles nor the people now had the skill or the resources to build
anything for the goddess much better than their own mud brick
houses. So the first temples looked no more imposing than this:

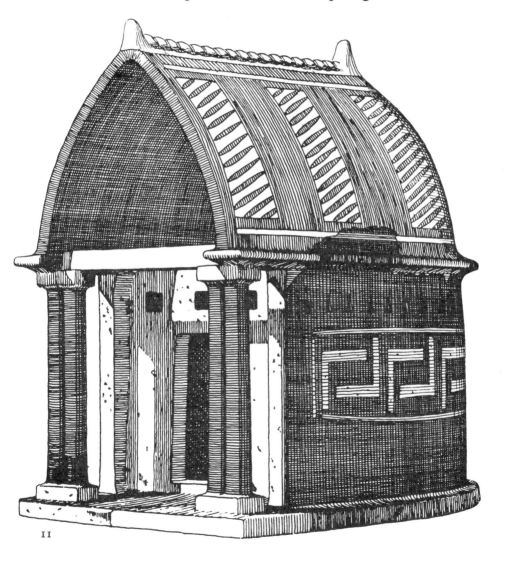

11

Being made of rubble and clay, with a mud or thatched roof, these temples have not survived, but there are clay models of them which have. (In this model the maker has painted wavy lines on the roof to show that the real roof was thatched.)

The brick and timber temples

Nevertheless memories of the stupendous palaces of the past that had once looked down on the Mycenaean towns from their grim citadels were kept alive by the songs and the stories that passed down from generation to generation, and by the sight of the massive ruins which were still visible, though half-buried in the debris of centuries. The great hall – called the *megaron* – of the mighty king to whom the people had turned for protection may have seemed a better example than their own insignificant houses of what the home of a goddess, or god, should look like. So the first temples that begin to look like classical temples are long and narrow, like the Mycenaean palace halls. This is the ground plan, revealed by excavation, of an early temple built for the goddess Hera (the wife of Zeus) on the island of Samos. It was 21 feet wide and 100 feet long. One end was quite

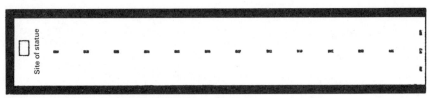

12a *Ground plan of the first temple of Hera.*

open, the other end and the two sides were built of sun-dried bricks. Down the middle there was a row of wooden columns which supported the roof. In front of the open end stood the altar. Later the worshippers had a colonnade of wooden columns added, right round the outside. Perhaps this was so that the roof could be extended and the brick walls protected from rain; or perhaps it was merely to look more impressive. There were seventeen columns along the sides and seven columns at the front and back. Half a century later the whole temple was destroyed – we do not know how – and a new temple was built on the same site. In the new temple the line of columns that went down the middle of the old temple was not rebuilt. Instead, the roof was supported by two rows of wooden columns set against the inside of the side walls. The new temple had a colonnade of eighteen columns along either side, six columns at the

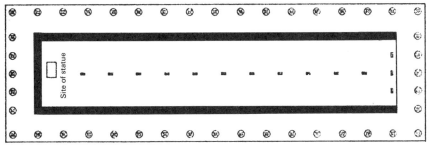

12b *Ground plan of the temple of Hera with columns added.*

front and rear, and between the six front columns and the entrance
to the central hall there was a second row of four columns. The
front now had two rows of columns and a gap between the centre
columns through which it was possible to look right into the dark
hall towards the statue of the goddess where she sat or perhaps stood
against the centre of the back wall of her *naos*. Previously the statue
had to be placed awkwardly to one side, otherwise she would have
been stuck directly behind a pillar. Now she could look straight out
to see what was going on at her altar. This is the ground plan.

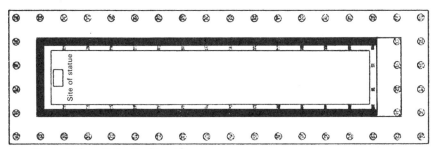

12c *Ground plan of the final temple.*

These three temples were on the same site and were built of
brick, rubble and timber on a stone platform.

From timber to stone
At some time after 700 BC the Greeks began building temples of
stone. These temples are the first of which more than the foundations
still survive. This is hardly surprising, since no timber is going to
last 2,700 years without rotting (a few wooden pillars seem to have
lasted as much as 1,000 years), whereas stone, if not tampered with

by human beings, is very durable when overthrown by an earthquake, as frequently happened in Greece.

With the first stone temples two different styles of building appeared. These were the Ionic and the Doric. The Ionic style was used by the Greeks of the islands and Asia Minor – those who had fled from the mainland at the time of the invasions and called themselves Ionians. The Doric style was used in western Greece, and in Sicily and southern Italy, where the invaders, who called themselves Dorians, had sent their colonies. Some experts say that the decoration on a Doric temple (the triglyphs, and metopes and the capitals of the columns) are a direct imitation in *stone* of features necessary to a *timber* building (like an electric fire that has sham coals which glow and flicker). Other experts say that this is nonsense and if you tried to put the beam ends where the triglyphs come on a stone temple you would soon get into difficulties. Whichever group of experts is right it is at least clear that some of the features of a wooden temple were imitated or adapted to create the decoration for the masonry that went between the top of the columns and the roof.

The columns
The stone columns themselves must have been imitated from wooden columns made from tree trunks. The simplest and quickest way to shape a tree trunk is to cut grooves all round it from end to end using an adze – a tool with a rounded blade. In a country of bright sunlight, these grooves (called 'fluting') will create attractive effects of light and shadow as the sun moves round the sky. In stone the grooves can be cut more sharply to give even finer effects.

The capitals of the columns are explained as being an imitation of the way in which the timber pillars were protected from water seeping into the grain. As the tree trunk dies, cracks are likely to appear at the ends, and if water gets into these it could seep down and rot the heart of the trunk. This could be prevented by covering it with a slice off the foot of the tree, topped by a slab of wood placed on its side so that the grain ran horizontally. As well as protecting the pillar from moisture this would help to distribute the thrust of the column over more of the lintel which it was supporting. On a Doric capital the *echinus* and the *abacus* are an imitation of this device.

The beams
In the wooden temples the lintels must have been massive beams lying across the tops of the pillars to hold up the framework of the

13

roof. Resting on these at right angles there would have been roof beams running from the front to the rear of the temple. The ends of these too would have needed to be protected by slabs of wood, and between them there would have been a gap which could have been closed by a wooden panel. These two features could have been the origin of the triglyphs and metopes of the Doric temple.

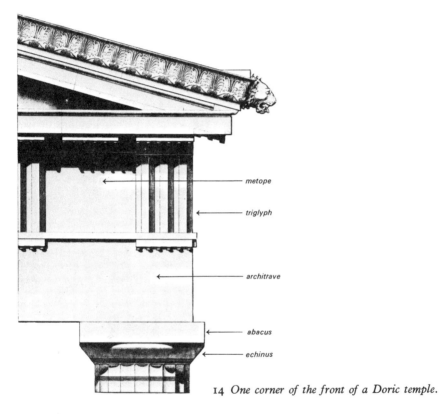

metope

triglyph

architrave

abacus

echinus

14 *One corner of the front of a Doric temple.*

Early stone temples and later developments
The surviving remains of early stone temples seem clumsy and unnecessarily solid, as if the builders did not trust the columns to bear the heavy weight of the stone superstructure. From 650 BC to 550 BC the designs were steadily refined and each element came nearer and nearer to perfection. The middle of the fifth century – the most creative period in all Greek history – produced what was undoubtedly one of the most beautiful buildings of all time, the Parthenon.

CHAPTER FOUR

From classical Greece to Imperial Rome

The beginnings of Rome

When the Athenians were busy building the Parthenon and the temple of Victorious Athena, the Romans were engaged in a long and difficult war to capture the little Etruscan town of Veii which was only 12 miles away from Rome. They had recently driven out their king, Tarquin the Proud, and turned themselves into a republic. Now there were bitter disputes between the nobles (patricians) who held all the power, and the other citizens (plebeians) who were demanding a share in it. These disputes hampered the conduct of the war but eventually the Romans captured Veii under the leadership of a patrician named Camillus. Five years later they suffered a disastrous defeat from an army of plundering Gauls and had to abandon Rome to be pillaged and burnt. Only the Capitol (the Roman acropolis) could be successfully defended. This too was nearly surprised in a night attack, but at the last moment (so the story goes) the garrison was roused by the cackling of a flock of geese (which the pious defenders had not eaten, though short of food, because they were sacred to the goddess Juno). The Gauls were driven off and eventually, on payment of a ransom, they withdrew to northern Italy, leaving Rome a smoking ruin. Veii, on the other hand, was still standing and many Romans, especially the plebeians, wanted to abandon Rome and transfer the entire population and all its possessions there.

The stories of early Rome are mostly legends which grew up in later years. They are full of difficulties overcome and disasters retrieved. The Romans were a sturdy and masterful people, and were destined to teach the world much about military tactics and organisation, about the administration of an empire, about law and engineering. But in religion and architecture they borrowed most of their practices from the Greeks and Etruscans.

Roman religion : the first beginnings

The Greeks, as we have seen, worshipped gods who were rather like outsize human beings. The early Romans were less inclined to worship gods with human shapes and human personalities. They gave some sort of worship to all the objects and influences that affected their lives, from the door they used to go out and come in by to the blight that destroyed their vines; from the cupboard where they kept their household stores, to the good or bad fortune that gave them victory or defeat in war; from the fire on their hearth to the ability of their flocks or their womenfolk to give birth. Everything had a mysterious power, neither good nor bad in itself, but capable of becoming either. All these objects and influences were therefore to be worshipped in whatever way would bring good results. Religious wisdom consisted in knowing what acts or words or offerings – or what combination of all three of these – had been found by previous generations to produce the best results. If these rites of worship were performed correctly then all would be well. If they were not performed at all things could go very wrong, but to perform them incorrectly was equally dangerous, and rather like messing around with high voltage electricity. If the rites were performed correctly and things *still* went wrong, then some divine power must have been involved which had, through ignorance, been neglected. In this case the remedy for a private citizen was to consult one of the religious officials, but if the disaster were a public one the remedy was for the officials to consult the Sibylline books.

The Sibylline books

A Roman legend said that these books, which contained all the religious lore necessary to save Rome in all the crises of her history, were sold to Tarquin the Proud, the last king of Rome, by an aged prophetess called a sibyl. She offered nine volumes of her prophecies for a high price. Tarquin eventually bought three volumes for the same price after she had burnt the other six. They were placed in a stone chest beneath the temple of Jupiter on the Capitol, and looked after by a committee of religious officials who consulted them whenever the state was in danger. They were finally destroyed when the Capitol was set on fire at the time of the civil wars that took place during the last century of the Republic (that is to say the hundred years that ended thirty-one years before the birth of Christ).

The sibyl was connected with the Greek colony of Cumae in southern Italy and when the books were consulted the advice they usually gave was that the worship of Greek gods or goddesses should be introduced into Rome. Just before the sack of Rome by the Gauls there was a severe famine, so, on the advice of the Sibylline books, the Roman magistrates built a temple for three deities named Ceres, Liber and Libera. Because they protected the crops and the vines they came to be thought of as being the same as the Greek deities Demeter, Dionysus and Persephone, who were also protectors of crops and vines. When the Romans suffered other disasters and consulted the Sibylline books they were advised to build temples to Aesculapius (the Greek god of healing, Asklepios), to Mercurius (who resembled the Greek god Hermes sufficiently for the Romans to believe him to be the same god), and to Neptune (a sea god, and so easily identified with the Greek sea god Poseidon). Finally, towards the end of the terrible war against Hannibal and the Carthaginians, the Sibylline books instructed the magistrates to bring to Rome the very *un*-Roman worship of Cybele, the great mother-goddess of Phrygia, whose priests were eunuchs.

The Etruscans

The Etruscans, whose cities all lay to the north of Rome, were a mysterious people whose language still puzzles the scholars who try to decipher it. They were thought by the Greeks to have come to Italy from Asia Minor – but some scholars find this story hard to believe. The Etruscans were in turn the rulers, enemies, allies and subjects of the Romans, and from them the Romans acquired some of their customs and institutions. (The gladiatorial shows may have been one such custom, and some scholars have a suspicion that they may have developed from the practice of human sacrifice.) The Etruscans themselves had copied the Greeks in many things, and were great importers of Greek statues, Greek vases and Greek artists. Their religion seems to have been gloomy and haunted by the fear of death and of demons who tormented the souls of the dead. They cremated their dead and placed the ashes in urns which were left in chambers hollowed out of the rock in vast underground cities of the dead. These chambers were furnished with chairs, beds, vases, statuettes and other objects that the dead might need if they continued to 'live' in their tombs. The walls of the chambers were painted with vivid scenes of banquets, dancing, hunting and other everyday activities, and sometimes with grim scenes of an underworld inhabited by grotesque and alarming demons. In the ancient world the Etruscans were famous for the elaborate system they had developed for discovering the will of the gods by examining the livers of sacrificial animals. The Romans were impressed by this art and made use of it, but they must have considered it rather sinister as they forbade citizens to learn it and always called in soothsayers

15a *Front view of a Roman temple built on the Etruscan plan.*

ROMAE·ET·AVGVSTO·CAESARI·INV·F·PATRI·PATRIAE

15b *Side view of the same temple.*

(*haruspices*) from Etruria when they felt the need for it.

Of the last kings of Rome, two (both named Tarquin) were Etruscans. The banishment of the last of these (Tarquin the Proud) was the cause of the wars of the Romans against the Etruscan cities. The first Tarquin (Tarquin the Elder) had begun a great temple on the Capitol to be dedicated to Jupiter, Juno and Minerva. It was completed by Tarquin the Proud, but not actually dedicated until a year after his banishment, when the ceremony was performed by one of the earliest consuls. It was always known to later Romans as the temple of Jupiter Optimus Maximus (Jupiter the Best and Greatest). Patriotic Romans believed that from this temple Jupiter watched over the destiny of Rome, just as patriotic Athenians had believed that Athena had watched over the destiny of Athens from the Athenian Acropolis. When the temple of Jupiter Optimus Maximus was burnt down during the civil wars the Romans rebuilt it almost exactly as it had been before.

Etruscan temples

Etruscan temples were very like Greek temples but they differed in some respects. They were raised on a high platform and were approached by steps from the front only. The colonnade did not usually go round the rear of the temple, and at the sides the columns were often attached to the side walls, so the only open colonnade was at the front. Etruscan temples often contained three *cellae* (*cella* was the Latin word for *naos*) side by side for three divinities, as was the case in the Roman temples of Ceres, Liber and Libera and of Jupiter, Juno and Minerva.

Roman religion becomes more and more Greek

Nearly all the pagan religions were very tolerant of one another, and when a pagan came across the worship of a strange god he was quite likely to feel that this was merely one of the gods he already worshipped under a different name. When the Romans conquered the Greek cities of southern Italy and Sicily, they came to know classical Greek art and literature. They were quite dazzled by its splendour and wished to have an equally great literature of their own. Soon there were Roman epics, Roman tragedies and Roman comedies. Though their first efforts were clumsy, the Romans did, in the end, produce in Horace and Virgil two poets whose achievements rivalled Greek poetry. One of the effects of all this interest in Greek art and literature was the total identification of the Roman gods and goddesses with those of the Greeks and a widespread knowledge of Greek mythology. Not only were all the Roman gods now of Greek origin, but the story was told and believed that the Romans' own ancestors were – not Greeks; they despised the Greeks of their own day too much for that – but heroes who had escaped from Troy and made their way to Italy under the leadership of King Priam's cousin Aeneas.

Hellenistic Greece
It is not surprising that the Romans despised the Greeks of their day. The glorious fifth century had ended with the defeat of Athens in a long and bitter war with Sparta. Most of the other city states had become involved in the struggle, which had been made more bitter and complicated by civil wars that had broken out *within* several of the city states, including Athens. After the war patriotism and loyalty to the city and to the city's patron goddess were never as strong again. Seventy years later the Greek cities lost their independence to King Philip of Macedon, and to his son Alexander the Great. After Alexander's death his empire was divided up among his generals who made themselves kings of Macedon, Syria and Egypt. (Their kingdoms are usually referred to as the Hellenistic monarchies.) Many new cities were founded in the conquered lands and Greeks were encouraged to go and live in them and build their temples and worship there. But the citizens no longer looked to the patron goddess of the city in time of trouble. Help for the city was more likely to come from the court of the king who ruled at Pella in Macedon, at Antioch in Syria, at Pergamos or Sardis in Asia Minor, or at Alexandria in Egypt, than from any god or human who lived in the building on the citadel.

Religious practice
From the end of the wars against Hannibal more and more of the Roman nobility were educated to speak and read Greek as fluently as Latin, and they were brought up on Greek literature and mythology. Nevertheless Roman religion was never quite the same as Greek religion. The Romans liked to have everything in their business dealings, in their politics and in the treaties they had with other cities clearly spelled out in precise phrases such as are used in legal documents. In the same way they thought of religion as a sort of business deal between gods and men which had to be set out in very careful language and carried out in very careful rituals. When the early Romans first came from their farms to live in the city and left the country life behind, they still went on performing the rituals intended to make sure that the sowing and harvesting were successful and that their vines were not damaged by blight. After a time these rituals

must have ceased to have any meaning for the city-dwellers, but they still went on with them.

Religion and patriotism

The early success of the Romans was largely due to the great patriotism and sense of duty of both common people and nobles. It was believed that if the commander of an army dedicated both himself and the enemy to the gods and then made sure that he was killed, the gods would be bound to take the enemy as well by destroying them. On two occasions, in desperate moments of battle, Roman generals uttered the solemn phrases dedicating themselves and the enemy and then rushed to certain death. In both cases victory was snatched from defeat and by the heroic action of the general (or so it seemed) the enemy, instead of winning, was utterly defeated.

The decadence of the nobles

During the last century of the Republic (which came to an end in 30 BC) patriotism and self-sacrifice were forgotten. As a result of the conquest of the Hellenistic kingdoms great wealth came to Rome and many slaves. This wealth made most of the nobles and the businessmen very rich indeed, but the poor remained very poor. Instead of taking pride in serving their country, most of the nobles now came to believe that only wealth and power were worth striving for. Few of them still believed seriously in the official religion and they shamelessly used religious customs and laws to trick their opponents. A few nobles who tried to reform the state were assassinated, and these assassinations began a century of bloodshed during which violence and massacres occurred every few years, as one group of nobles or another succeeded in capturing power and having their enemies put to death. During this period the buildings on the Capitol were burnt down and the temples all over Rome were allowed to fall into decay – except for the temple of Jupiter Optimus Maximus, which was too important to be neglected even in time of disorder. Many acts of sacrilege were committed. Roman generals looted temples in conquered countries to pay their troops, or carried off statues of the gods to decorate their own luxurious villas. When a group seized power they did not hesitate to put members of their own family to death if they had been supporting the other side, and defeated politicians who had taken refuge at an altar were dragged away to be killed.

The Roman priesthoods

Like the Greek priests the Roman priests were officials of the state, elected by the people; but there were no family priesthoods, as there were in Greece. Unlike the Greek priests the Roman priests did not have particular temples to look after but supervised all the official worship of the state. They were organised into committees (or boards), each of which attended to a particular part of the state worship. The head of them all was the *Pontifex Maximus* (High Priest). This office brought great honour and influence. Julius Caesar, long before he had become famous as a general, got himself elected Pontifex Maximus, defeating two distinguished and much older nobles, by spending vast sums of money on bribery. He knew it would help him in his political career. The orator and politician Cicero was elected one of the augurs. These were priests whose duties were to make sure that any signs in the sky (such as thunder or lightning, or flocks of birds) which might reveal the will of the gods were properly interpreted and noted. He was very proud of holding this priesthood, although he did not himself believe in the gods.

A special feature of Roman religion was the worship of Vesta. Vesta was the goddess of all family hearths, but in particular she was the goddess of the state hearth of the city of Rome. This hearth was in a temple specially built for it in the centre of Rome – the Temple of Vesta. The fire was ceremonially lit on the first day of March every year by the Pontifex Maximus, and it was tended with the utmost care by the Vestal Virgins, the priestesses of Vesta. These were chosen between the ages of six and ten and taken away from their families. Their heads were shaved and they were placed under the care of the Pontifex Maximus, who became their official 'father' for the whole of their time as Vestal Virgins. This began with ten years of training in their duties, which were many. Apart from tending the fire and making a small offering of food every day on the hearth on behalf of the city, they performed various ceremonial duties, as well as practical functions such as looking after the wills of important people. They were always treated with very great respect. They had to serve for thirty years, after which they were allowed to resign and marry. If a Vestal Virgin took a lover before it was time for her to resign, she was condemned to be buried alive and her lover was flogged to death. It was believed that her action placed the state in great danger.

Greek and Roman sacrifices
There were several differences in the way Greeks and Romans made a sacrifice. In a Greek sacrifice the priest stood with his head bare, in a Roman sacrifice the priest covered his head with a fold of his toga. The Romans had a flute player to play throughout the ceremony

so that no sound that might be thought to forbode ill should reach the ears of the worshippers. The Romans also frequently used Etruscan *haruspices* to examine the liver of the animals in order to foretell future events. Emperors were sometimes warned by *haruspices* of their imminent assassination, but of course it could not do them any good – otherwise the *haruspices* would have been proved wrong. Unlike Greek temples, Roman temples sometimes had altars in the portico, and the public were admitted into the *cella* to make vows or offer incense more often than they were into the *naos* of a Greek temple. The Romans often used temples for meetings of the Senate, whereas temples were not used for political meetings by the Greeks. Finally there was a custom that was said to have originated with the Greeks but which they practised very rarely, while the Romans practised it often. This was the *lectisternium*. In this cere-mony the statues of the gods were brought out from the temples and laid on couches in full view of the public to be garlanded and pre-sented with offerings. The Romans were first instructed to do this by the Sibylline books at a moment of crisis during the siege of Veii, when famine and pestilence had been added to their difficulties.

The downfall of the gods and their survival

The temple of Jupiter the Best and Greatest

In early Rome the new year began on 1 March. The first meeting of the Senate after that date was always held in the temple of Jupiter on the Capitol, even after the date of the New Year had been changed to 1 January. On this date the new consuls for the year put on their purple-bordered togas and went in procession to the temple of Jupiter to sacrifice white bulls as a sign of the state's gratitude for its preservation during the past year, in accordance with vows made by the previous consuls. They then made fresh vows and took their seats for the first time on their ceremonial thrones in front of the temple to the cheers of the crowd. After this they returned, again in procession, to hold a meeting of the Senate.

It was to the temple of Jupiter that every general went to make his vows before setting off on a campaign, and to the temple of Jupiter he returned to pay his vows if he came home victorious.

The anniversary of the first dedication of the temple in 507 BC fell on 13 September, and each year on that day a white cow was sacrificed to Jupiter by one of the consuls, and all the senators and magistrates sat down to a banquet in the temple. Special couches were brought and on these were placed the statues of Jupiter, Juno and Minerva, all dressed in fine clothes as if they were guests of honour at the banquet.

These were not the only occasions when the temple of Jupiter was the focus for an event in the calendar of Roman ceremonials, but they show how important a place it occupied in the public life of Rome and in the thoughts of ordinary Roman citizens, who felt that Jupiter in his temple perched above the centre of the city watched over their safety. The politician Cicero once made a speech to announce that he had crushed a conspiracy which might have led to a new outbreak of civil war. He proclaimed that it was not he who had crushed the conspiracy, but Jupiter himself, in order to protect 'the Capitol, these temples, the whole city and all of you'. Cicero knew that the Roman people would listen eagerly to this sort of oratory, though he himself cannot have believed a word of it.

Augustus and the temples of Rome

Rome's terrible century of cruelty, bloodshed and disorder ended in 30 BC with the victory of Octavian (the nephew and heir of Julius Caesar) over all his enemies. He became sole ruler (although Rome remained in name a republic) and took the title of Augustus. In his rise to power he had been as murderous as anyone, but now his object was peace, harmony, firm government and reverence for the ancient glory and customs of Rome. The revival of the state religion was an important part of his political programme, and he secured the help of the leading poets, Virgil and Horace, to proclaim in their poetry a new age of peace, prosperity and piety. He organised a great building programme to repair the old temples and to construct new ones. It was carried out so magnificently that he could boast that he had found Rome built of brick but left her built of marble.

The Vestal and the Pontifex

By now it may be a little clearer why the priest and the silent virgin, in the poem by Horace, were climbing the citadel (the *Capitolium*), and who they were. They were almost certainly about to offer sacrifice at the temple of Jupiter Optimus Maximus, and the silent virgin was almost certainly a Vestal, perhaps the senior Vestal. One might have supposed that the priest Horace had in mind was the Pontifex Maximus, but this seems unlikely. At the time this poem was written the Pontifex Maximus was an ex-politician and unsuccessful general, born of an ancient and distinguished family, named Marcus Aemilius Lepidus, and he was living in comfortable banishment from Rome in the little seaside town of Circeii. After the assassination of Julius Caesar, Octavian had made a temporary alliance with Lepidus and Mark Antony against the murderers of Caesar. When these had been defeated and Lepidus was no longer necessary or useful, Octavian deprived him of his army and banished him for the rest of his life to Circeii. However, part of the original bargain had been that Lepidus should become Pontifex Maximus in place of the dead Caesar, and the election had been duly rigged. Because this was a religious office to be held for life, Octavian (now Augustus) did not deprive him of it, as this would have made a mockery of the new policy of reviving respect for religious customs. Instead he waited until Lepidus died, and then had himself properly elected in his place. We can only suppose that while Lepidus was alive and in banishment his duties in Rome were carried out by one of the other *pontifices*, deputising for him.

The speech of Camillus

The historian Livy was another author who in his writings supported Augustus' attempts to revive admiration for the heroism of Rome's early struggles. Livy's history of Rome's rise to greatness is full of deeds of bravery and patriotism and stirring speeches. One such speech is concerned with the proposal to remove Rome from its site on the seven hills beside the River Tiber and establish it elsewhere. Ever since the time of Julius Caesar's dictatorship there had been rumours that Rome might be abandoned and a new capital established in the eastern Mediterranean, perhaps by rebuilding the site of Troy. Then, when Mark Antony divided the Roman world with Octavian and set up his headquarters in Egypt with Cleopatra, the Romans feared that Alexandria might become the new capital. When he was defeated by Octavian, rumours persisted that Octavian now might take up the idea. Both Livy and Horace warned against it. Horace in one of his poems made the goddess Juno prophesy that Roman power and the Roman Capitol would prosper only as long as Troy remained a ruin. Livy, telling of the proposal to move from Rome to Veii, made after the sack of Rome by the Gauls, put a passionate speech into the mouth of Camillus, the general who had captured Veii, in which he opposed any such plan:

'Vanquished . . . we fled for refuge to the *Capitolium*, to the house of Jupiter Best and Greatest. . . . Abandoned by gods and men, yet we did not forget the rites of holy worship. As a result the gods have restored to us our country, victory and our former glory in war. We are in possession of a city . . . in which there is not a spot which is not sanctified by worship and the presence of gods. . . . Do you intend, O Romans, to forsake all these divinities, both public and private? . . . Can the festival of Jupiter be performed anywhere else than on the *Capitolium*? . . . O Vesta, shall thy virgins forsake thee?'

The downfall of the gods

However 350 years later Constantine the Great did abandon both Rome and the pagan religion and moved the capital of the Roman Empire – not to Veii, but to Constantinople, which was not far from the site of ancient Troy. Constantinople flourished for another eleven centuries, while Rome was sacked by one barbarian army after another. Pagans said this was a punishment for closing the temples and abandoning the age-old sacrifices to the gods. Paganism lingered on for many years, especially in the countryside, but after a time

Christianity was accepted by all the peoples of the former Roman Empire, though less than 400 years after Constantine most of the inhabitants of the eastern and African provinces became Mohammedans.

The survival of the gods

In the Dark Ages and the Middle Ages Christians did not so much disbelieve in the existence of the gods of Greece and Rome, as think of them as evil demons liable to terrify and torment them. Apollo became the foul fiend Apollyon, and the horned and goat-legged god Pan became the image in which the devil himself appeared to tempt or frighten Christians. It could be said that gods continue to exist as long as people believe in them, and that astrologers who give the names and the characters of the pagan gods to the planets, and believe that they influence human destiny, have kept them alive to this day.

The influence of Greek and Roman architecture

In the later Middle Ages returning prosperity and the revival of intellectual curiosity made possible a serious interest in the religion, mythology, art and architecture of the Greeks and Romans. Rich and important men paid large sums for the naked statues which had formerly been thought wicked. Farm labourers working in the fields, when they happened to dig up masterpieces which had been

16 *A terrace in Regent's Park, London, built in neo-classical style.*

17 (opposite) *A house in South Carolina, USA, with a pediment and portico of Ionic columns.*

buried beneath the ruins of ancient villas, now sold them instead of destroying them. These statues were copied by artists, who took also to burrowing their way into the ruins of Roman palaces and copying any paintings they found still visible on the walls. So came Renaissance art, which devoted as much time and talent to illustrating stories from Roman legends and Greek mythology as to glorifying the saints and illustrating the stories of Christianity. The architecture of this period was influenced mostly by the architecture of the Romans, but two centuries later Greek architecture came into its own with the neo-classical movement, which began at the end of the eighteenth century. Teams of architects were paid by wealthy men to go to Greece and Turkey to draw the ruins of any buildings they could find. (Some of the drawings in this book were made in this way.) This is the period when some of the sculptures from the Parthenon were brought to the British Museum, and when many churches in England and Scotland were built in imitation of Greek temples. Houses and whole city squares were decorated with pillars and pilasters copied from Greek architecture. In America, too, wealthy men built themselves magnificent residences of timber (because timber was plentiful but stone scarce). These had colonnaded porticos and pediments in the Ionic or Doric style. So once again pillars and architraves and pediments were being built in timber, as they had been in the very beginning.

FURTHER STUDY

A The orders of architecture
B The Parthenon
C Other types of temple and other forms of worship
D Some differences between pagan and Christian worship
E How to learn more about Greek and Roman religion and
    temple architecture and their later influence

FURTHER STUDY A

THE ORDERS OF ARCHITECTURE

Doric and Ionic
For about three centuries there were two styles of temple architecture
among the Greeks, Doric and Ionic. Then an architect invented a new
style, the Corinthian, and about four centuries later the Romans added
two more. The Doric and Ionic developed in separate parts of the Greek
world: the Doric in western Greece and in the Greek colonies in Sicily
and southern Italy; the Ionic in the islands of the Aegean Sea and in the
colonies founded on or near the coasts of Asia Minor. The Athenians
were between these two areas and used both styles. The Doric was so
called because most of the Greeks of the west spoke the Dorian (or Doric)
dialect of Greek; and the Ionic style received its name because in the
colonies where it developed the Ionian (or Ionic) dialect was spoken.

The columns
First and foremost the difference between the two styles is in the columns.
    The Doric column has no base. It stands on the same platform as the
rest of the temple. The capital (top) of the column is very simple, like
this:

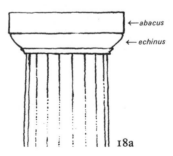

←abacus
←echinus

18a

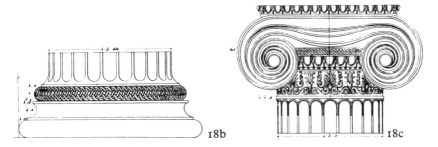

18b

18c

The Ionic column stands on a bulging base (18b). Its capital (18c) is more elaborate than the Doric capital.

Both columns have fluting, but whereas the twenty channels in the Doric fluting meet in a sharp ridge, with Ionic fluting there is a flat-topped ridge between each of the twenty-four channels and the next, as you can see in the two pictures above. Ionic columns were also slimmer than Doric columns.

It may well be asked why the column came to play such a very big part in Greek temple building. The answer could be simply that Ancient Greece was very wooded, and that in a timber construction a tree trunk is a very handy means of supporting a roof. Another answer could be that trees were worshipped in the primitive religions of the Mediterranean, and the sanctity of trees had been transferred to columns from very early times (there is evidence that they were worshipped in the pre-Greek civilisations), so that it seemed very appropriate to surround the house of a god with beautiful columns.

Entablature
This word is used to describe everything the architect puts between the top of the column and the roof.

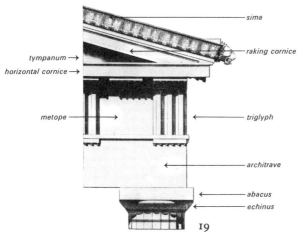

sima

raking cornice

tympanum →
horizontal cornice →

metope

triglyph

architrave

abacus
echinus

19

(a) Doric : with the Doric order the architect almost invariably followed the same arrangement. This was: (1) sima; (2) raking cornice; (3) tympanum; (4) horizontal cornice; (5) frieze, consisting of alternate triglyph and metope; (6) architrave. Very little variation was allowed. The architect could, and often did, put sculpture between the horizontal cornice and the raking cornice. He could also chose various ways of decorating the sima.

(b) Ionic : The Ionic horizontal cornice was decorated and the architrave often consisted of three slim slabs of stone where the Doric was one massive block. The pediment was shallower and did not contain any sculpture.

Comparisons between Doric and Ionic
Ancient writers used to say that the Doric style was masculine and the Ionic feminine, by which they probably meant that the Doric gave an impression of strength, while the Ionic gave an impression of grace. In several temples, especially at Athens, the two styles were mixed, the exterior of the temple being Doric while the roof of the *naos* was supported by Ionic columns.

Corinthian columns
At the end of the fifth century BC an architect was impressed by the sight of an acanthus (a Greek type of thistle with large leaves which in England can be seen in the garden of the Roman palace at Fishbourne) growing round a basket that had been placed as an offering on a grave. He substituted a decoration derived from this for the capital of an Ionic column, and the result became very fashionable. It largely replaced the two older styles of capital in buildings constructed after the time of Alexander the Great.

Roman columns
The Romans took over the Greek styles, preferring the Corinthian; but they also used a mixture of the Ionic and Corinthian capitals (known as the composite order), as well as a Tuscan order, which was merely a plain form of Doric. (This can be seen in the Roman palace at Fishbourne.)

20 *Corinthian.*

21 *Composite.*

FURTHER STUDY B

THE PARTHENON

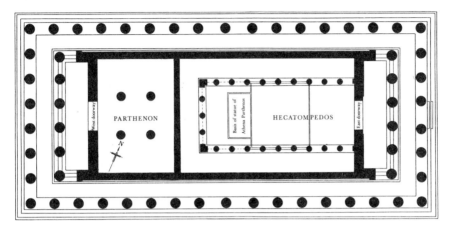

22 *Plan of the Parthenon.*

It has been claimed that the Parthenon was the most beautiful building ever constructed. You may well ask what was so wonderful about it, if all Doric temples were very much alike. The answer seems to be three things: the site, the sculptures and the great subtlety of all its lines and proportions. It has been said that there is not one single straight line in the whole building, from front to back or from top to bottom. This is not strictly true, but the curve of the platform and the subtle irregularities of the columns create a sense of living tension which makes any perfectly regular building look lifeless and too solid by contrast.

Then there is the extraordinary beauty of the ornamental sculpture, designed and in part carried out by Phidias. Added to this is the high degree of skill and finish in all the smallest details of the construction. To produce such a result, the work force must have contained skilled men who had already worked under Phidias on a similar temple at Olympia, while all the workers, whether slaves, resident foreigners or citizens, dedicated themselves with enthusiasm to their part of the task, however humble. Mention should also be made of the high quality of the materials: marble from Mount Pentelicon, cedar for the roof, and gold and ivory for the statue of the goddess.

Finally there is the site itself. This was not given by nature, but was the result of building up one area of the Acropolis into a platform for the perfect display of a masterpiece. But the display is not formal. The Parthenon is not on the centre of the Acropolis, nor did it stand above a city laid out with wide streets in geometric lines like the cities planned by the Romans. The Greek town planners believed in adapting the new to the old and not trying to straighten out what had grown up haphazardly. The Roman style is more imposing, but the Greek style is more refreshing to the eye. (Modern ideas of town planning are beginning to show signs of reverting at last to Greek practice in this.)

Plutarch

The Greek writer Plutarch, who was born about AD 46, wrote about the Parthenon and the other buildings on the Acropolis as they were in his own day – 500 years after they were built. He said that even then each one seemed as if it had only just been finished: 'They keep their fresh appearance, untouched by time, as if an ageless spirit breathed in them.'

23 Sculptures from the east frieze of the Parthenon.

FURTHER STUDY C

OTHER TYPES OF TEMPLE AND OTHER FORMS OF WORSHIP

Olympia and Delphi

In this book shortage of space has obliged us to confine ourselves to one kind of temple and form of worship – that of the great patron gods and goddesses of the cities. Besides these there were other temples to the Olympian gods in which worship was not confined to the citizens of any one city. At Olympia there was a temple to Zeus, in whose honour the Olympic games were held. The games were a festival to which Greeks from all over the Greek world came – and not only Greeks, though only Greeks could compete. The temple of Zeus was for all who came to Olympia, and it received many offerings from those who came to watch or to compete.

At Delphi, Apollo received worship from pilgrims. These came to ask advice from the priests who interpreted the words of the inspired priestess who gave prophetic replies from the oracular shrine. As well as a temple, there was a theatre at Delphi and a stadium where games were held in honour of Apollo. These games became almost as famous as the Olympic games.

Humble worship
Apollo and Zeus were Olympian gods, very mighty and magnificent. The ordinary Greek townsman or small farmer felt more at home worshipping at the shrine of some humbler local hero or nymph, who would not be busy ruling the earth and heavens, and so might have more time to help the poor and insignificant – just as many poor Italians today pray to their local saint rather than to God.

Oriental religions
Alexander the Great and his successors founded new cities all over Asia Minor in lands that had been part of the great Persian Empire. They persuaded Greeks to come to live in these cities and to organise them just like Greek cities. However a large part of the population was oriental, and new religions, which had grown out of oriental beliefs, became very popular with these mixed populations. Later these religions spread westwards to Greece and Italy, and especially to Rome where an increasing proportion of the population was descended from slaves, many of them of oriental origin. Most of these religions had full-time priests (who were sometimes eunuchs, like the priests of Cybele from Phrygia mentioned on page 42), and part of the worship was often secret. A different style of temple was needed with space for the secret worship to take place where it could not be seen by people who did not belong to that particular religious community.

The most important of these religions were the worship of Isis, the worship of Sarapis and the worship of Mithras. Isis was an Egyptian goddess, Sarapis was half-Greek and half-Egyptian, created by the Greek rulers of Egypt with the help of an Egyptian priest to provide a religion that could be shared by both their Greek and their Egyptian subjects. The worship of Mithras came originally from Persia. In the second century AD it spread widely in the Roman Empire, especially among the soldiers. Temples of Mithras were found at many of the garrison towns of the Roman frontier. There was at least one in London, and there are many monuments of Mithraic religion along Hadrian's Wall.

These religions were in many ways closer to Christianity – which itself came to the Roman Empire as an oriental religion from Judaea – than they were to the state religions of the Greeks and Romans. They had an organised priesthood, they were not controlled by the state, and they were more concerned with life after death than the state religions were.

FURTHER STUDY D

SOME DIFFERENCES BETWEEN CHRISTIAN AND PAGAN WORSHIP

Churches and temples

(a) Churches

The original name for a church is the Greek word *ecclesia* which means 'a place of assembly'. The very earliest Christian churches were rooms in private houses. Gradually, as more and more people were converted to Christianity, it became necessary to have a special building where the larger congregations could meet. By the time Christianity became the official religion of the Roman Empire, Roman architects had discovered how to use concrete to build vast and imposing buildings of immense strength. These were quite plain outside but their interiors were made impressive and beautiful with richly coloured mosaics on the walls and ceilings. Such buildings – huge halls in the imperial palaces for the emperor to appear in state to his courtiers, or magnificent public baths which emperors built to make themselves popular in the great cities of the empire, or massive law courts – were imitated by the architects of the first big Christian churches. They used the opportunities for decoration to proclaim on the walls and ceilings the glory of Christ in his heavenly kingdom, and the message that what mattered to the good Christian was not the happenings of this world, but the life that awaited him in heaven after death, or after the end of the world, which the early Christians expected to come quite soon. In later churches this message is often conveyed in elaborate stained glass windows, which are the glory of many medieval churches and cathedrals.

(b) Temples

Temples, as we have seen, were not built to contain a congregation. The congregation remained outside. Though there are exceptions (such as the secretive oriental cults), it can be stated without too much exaggeration that whereas everything that is important to a Christian takes place *inside* a church, everything that was important to a pagan took place *outside* a temple. This is neatly illustrated by the procedure followed by Christian architects when they took over a Greek temple, as they sometimes did, to make it into a church. They turned it inside out by filling in the spaces between the columns on the outside, and cutting wide openings in the walls of the *naos* inside, to make a nave with aisles. Naturally all the main decoration of the temple was *outside*. This decoration did not carry any message about life after death or of other religious beliefs. It was usually intended solely as beautiful and pleasing ornamentation, and consisted of vivid scenes from mythology, not necessarily connected with the god or goddess to whom the temple was dedicated.

Another difference is that from the earliest times the Christian churches had a social function, as a centre for the care of all the Christians living in the area. Even now, when social care has been largely taken over by the state, each church serves a parish, so you do not see churches clustered together in a group. In the pagan religion there were no parishes, and temples were often grouped where there was a specially holy site.

Altars

We have seen how important the altar was in pagan worship. In the very earliest days of Christianity the Christian altar was no more than a wooden table suitable for the ritual of the communion service, in which the congregation commemorates the last supper Christ took with his disciples. When the first churches were built, the Christians began to have stone altars. They were often hollow, like coffins, and contained the bones and other relics of martyred Christians. These altars became the focal point of the church. But they were so different from the bloodstained pagan altars that early Christians often denied that they had altars at all.

Priests

The word priest comes from a Greek word meaning 'elder'. The early Christian priests were simply responsible members of the congregation who helped to organise the worship. However, in time the Christian church became more and more organised into a tightly knit institution devoted, in intention if not always in practice, to preserving spiritual and civilised values in a violent, lawless and wicked world. Then the priest became a man set apart from other men by a consecration which symbolised Christ's choice of his twelve apostles. After about 1100 AD the Catholic priests who were controlled by the Pope (but not the Orthodox priests of the Byzantine Empire) were expected to remain unmarried. They also wore clothes that distinguished them from ordinary people. They were, and are, trained in religious doctrine and one of their duties is to teach it. Until about a century ago almost all secondary education in England was conducted by priests.

The Greek priest (*hiereus*), as we have seen, was no more than an ordinary citizen who needed to know only the ritual of his own particular temple. He played no part in education, and his duties probably took up no more time than do those of a town councillor in any small town today. The Roman priest (*sacerdos*), as we have also seen, could be an atheist and a very active politician.

FURTHER STUDY E

HOW TO LEARN MORE ABOUT GREEK AND ROMAN RELIGION AND TEMPLE ARCHITECTURE, AND THEIR LATER INFLUENCE

1. Look around the town where you live for examples on buildings of Doric, Ionic and Corinthian columns. Sketch them, or photograph them,

or make notes about them. Find out when the buildings were constructed and work out why the architect may have chosen to copy this particular style for his building. There is plenty of bad architecture about and the reason may well be a bad one. For example, the architect could have imagined that it would make a cheap building look more classy than it was; or he may have wanted to give the customers of some commercial firm the feeling that the firm was far too dignified to cheat them; or he may have wished to inspire awe in simple people by making his building very different from their own simple dwellings. But there could well be very good reasons. You will notice that, in addition to the proper columns that support a roof or porch, there are engaged columns which stand against a wall, and pilasters which are only half-columns or quarter-columns attached to a wall. Often these are not supporting anything, but are there merely for decoration.

2. Find out what happened to the Parthenon between the time of Constantine the Great and Lord Elgin, and make up your mind whether the 'Elgin marbles' (the sculptures Lord Elgin brought from the Parthenon to the British Museum) ought to be returned to Athens.

3. If you have Jewish, Muslim or Hindu friends, ask them (very tactfully, as some people do not like talking about their religion) what happens at their place of worship. Compare their answer with what you know of Greek and Roman temples and Christian churches. If you are Jewish, or Muslim or Hindu and have a Christian friend, find out more about Christian worship from him (or her) and make a similar comparison.

4. Imagine that you are a young Roman, and have inherited some property jointly with your brother. You have schemed to cheat him of his share by a clever legal trick and have made a vow that you will sacrifice a black ewe to Hecate if the trick succeeds. It does, and you now go to the temple to pay the vow. But everything goes wrong with the sacrifice and you are very frightened that you will regret what you have done. Describe the day on which you make the sacrifice. (All the necessary details can be found in the third chapter of a little book by R. M. Ogilvie called *The Romans and their Gods* (Chatto & Windus, 1970).)

5. The Ionic column that was placed at the corner of a porch or colonnade presented the architect with a problem. Try making a sketch and see what the problem was. Then find out how it was solved. (You may be able to see the solution on many Ionic columns in your own town.)

6. Imagine that you are an archaeologist in the year 3000 BC, and that the whole of the civilised world was devastated by some catastrophe in the period between AD 2000 and AD 2200. No books or written documents of any kind have survived. You have excavated a few churches and cathedrals, of which little more than the foundations remains, together

with some gravestones (which you can just decipher), a few relics of crucifixes and some pieces of stained glass which you have carefully pieced together. Write a scholarly report of a reconstruction of Christian beliefs and worship based on your finds.

7. On page 22 there is a story about the workman who fell when working on the sacred gateway to the Acropolis. Write an imaginative account of how the accident happened and how the other workmen felt about it. To make your story convincing you will have to find out some details of the gateway (called the Propylaea).

8. The Greek quotation at the beginning of this book comes from the sixth book of the *Iliad*. Read the passage it comes from (it is on page 125 of the Penguin translation, beginning 'When they reached the temple of Athene on the Acropolis . . .'), and compare it with this (written in 1972): '. . . you may see even today in some church in Naples a peasant woman appealing to the statue of the saint as if it were not stone or wood, but the saint himself, alive and listening.' Then write an account of the procession of the Trojan women to the temple of Athena, as it might have been described to you by one of the women.

9. This is quite a difficult exercise. On page 28 it was stated that a priest or priestess whose son or daughter died had to give up the priesthood. Try to think out what the Greeks must have felt about the gods and their dealings with mortals for them to have made this rule. Articles on Greek religion in encyclopedias or other books of reference will help you to make an intelligent guess.

24 *The remains of the Parthenon as they appeared at the beginning of the nineteenth century, when Athens was under Turkish rule.*